CORRECT ME IF I'M WRONG

A Practical Approach to Improving Written English

Rosemary Moor

Senior Lecturer in English and Study Skills,
Greenhill College, Harrow

Stanley Thornes (Publishers) Ltd

Text © Rosemary Moor 1988

Illustrations © Stanley Thornes (Publishers) Ltd 1988

First published in 1988 by:
Stanley Thornes (Publishers) Ltd
Old Station Drive
Leckhampton
CHELTENHAM GL53 0DN
England

British Library Cataloguing in Publication Data

Moor, Rosemary
    Correct me if I'm wrong: a practical
    approach to improving written English.
    1.   English language — Grammar —
    1950–
    I.   Title
    428.2   PE1112

    ISBN 0-85950-713-0

Typeset by Tech-Set, Gateshead, Tyne & Wear
Printed and bound in Great Britain at The Bath Press, Avon

Contents

Introduction

The material used in this book is taken from mistakes that constantly recur in pupils' written work. The language throughout is simple; technical terminology is kept to a minimum. The descriptive language used is based on function rather than category. For example, a clause is called a 'weak sentence' as opposed to a 'strong sentence'; a conjunction is called a 'weak' word. Understanding of the material comes by pupils talking and working through the exercises, rather than by lengthy written explanation.

HOW TO USE THIS BOOK

Pupils should preferably work in pairs or groups. The teacher can place a time limit of five or ten minutes to work an exercise. The pupils should talk through the material. A teacher-controlled plenary session can be introduced at any point, but this is rarely necessary. Pupils working together and groups checking against each other almost invariably find the correct answer. As they work through exercises, the pupils will do a lot of thinking and talking about punctuation, grammar, usage and spelling as they 'prove' to each other that their answer is right. Pupils should either copy out short exercises as suggested in the text or use photocopies. Exercises marked with an asterisk may be photocopied and can be found on the copyright-free worksheets at the end of the book. One photocopy between two pupils is a satisfactory arrangement.

Each part of *How a Sentence Works* requires detailed attention from the pupils. It should be worked on by pupils with specific problems, for instance, inability to recognise a sentence; or pupils in groups can work through the material. Only a limited amount should be undertaken each time. It is useful to intersperse parts of this chapter with work on other sections of the book.

Nine Rules of Punctuation can be used for quick reference by individual pupils or for effective group work. Where a group of pupils share the same type of punctuation problem – for example, not knowing how to use speech marks – they should work together through the explanations and exercises. Once the section has been completed, pupils use it for making corrections on all subsequent written work. For example, if the teacher writes '8' in the margin to indicate a mistake with speech marks, the pupil refers to Rule 8, finds the relevant explanation and makes the correction. This type of correcting, done in small groups, helps students learn the rules of punctuation.

The *Alphabetical List of Common Mistakes* can be used as a ready-reference guide. Pupils can quickly look up the correct usage in the case of ordinary mistakes in expression or spelling. Many pupils enjoy working through the exercises and discovering what is or is not standard usage. Teachers can use the code 'CM' in the margin when correcting pupils' work to refer them to the correct section of the book.

Some Rules of Usage shows how to correct more complicated mistakes, such as misuse of the conditional, problems of pronoun reference, etc. Pupils should concentrate on the section that refers directly to a mistake they have made, rather than work through the whole section from beginning to end. 'RU' written in the margin of a marked paper, refers the pupil to that section of the book.

In *Seven Suggestions for Better Spelling*, pupils should be encouraged to apply the suggestions, especially numbers 1 and 2. They should work on each suggestion for two or three weeks before starting another. The list of 50 words should be used as a reference for pupils who have trouble with particular words.

Note: Exercises marked with an asterisk may be photocopied. They are to be found on the copyright-free worksheets at the end of the book.

NOUNS

A *noun* is the name of something (a person, object, place, idea, etc.).

*WORKING IN PAIRS

This exercise can be found on Worksheet 1.

*CONTINUED PAIR WORK

This exercise can be found on Worksheet 1.

PRONOUNS

A *pronoun* is a word such as *I, my, mine, me, we, our, us, she, her, he, his, him, it, its, you, your, they, their, them*. These words are used instead of nouns so it isn't necessary to keep using the same noun over and over again. The pronoun usually refers back to some particular *noun* already mentioned.

poor: Jake went skiing for the first time last year. Jake liked skiing very much. Jake decided to get a job so that Jake could go skiing again.

better: Jake went skiing for the first time last year. *He* liked *it* very much. *He* decided to get a job so that *he* could go skiing again.

WORKING IN PAIRS

Write out the second example on page 1. Circle all the words that are
pronouns. *Draw a line connecting the* pronoun *to the* noun *it refers back to.*

VERBS

A *verb* shows action – either mental or physical action. A *verb* is often called a *doing* or a *being* word.

> *doing words*:   eat, sing, buy, think, love
> *being words*:   am, is, feel, seem, was

WORK THIS THROUGH

In the paragraph below, all the verbs are underlined.

The huge yew tree <u>gave</u> Mr Pepper the idea. He <u>decided</u> to <u>build</u> a tree-house – not for his children, but for himself. He <u>measured</u> the possible floor, that <u>is</u> branch, space, and <u>found</u> that the tree <u>allowed</u> for a three-floor house. Great, he <u>thought</u>, tomorrow a life-long dream <u>starts</u> to <u>become</u> a reality. Already I <u>feel</u> a part of nature.

Write out the paragraph and above each of the underlined <u>verbs</u>, *write whether it is a* <u>doing</u> *or a* <u>being verb</u>.

Verbs can be one *doing* word (see page 2), or they can be several words working together to form a verb group. It is important to learn to recognise the most common verbs that work together to form verb groups.

In the dialogue below several of these verb groups are underlined. Notice that some words are both circled and underlined.

Hilary: (Has) anyone seen my English book around?

Mother: I (can) not believe it! You (have) lost that book three times, not counting the one that (was) lost last week. You (ought to) have a place where you (can) put your books.

Hilary: I (could) put it in my room but it was on the dining room table. Someone (must have) moved it. I (was) writing a book report on it. What (shall) I do? It is terribly important.

Mother: I (will) help you look, but you are silly. If you had any sense, you (would) not leave it around. You (might) have to borrow the book from Jenny.

Hilary: I (am) not borrowing from her. She (is) annoyed with me already. We (are) hardly speaking. In fact we (have) had a terrible row.

Mother: (Did) you do something to cause it? You (should) be more careful about your friends. You (would) be in a bad way without them.

Hilary: Well, I (have) been rather stupid. She (does) have a right to be annoyed. The book I lost last week was hers.

WORK THIS THROUGH

Make a list of all the circled verbs above. These are called helping verbs. As you see, they can work in groups with doing or being verbs. It would be useful to get to know these helping verbs so that you can always spot them.

*WORKING IN PAIRS

This exercise can be found on Worksheet 2.

TENSE

The *tense* of the verb tells the time in which the action of the sentence takes place. Adding *ed* or *en* to a verb means the action is in the past; *s* means the present. The helping verbs also determine the time of the action.

✓ Ben *likes* the boy next door. (present time)
✓ Ben *liked* the boy next door. (past time)

✓ They *will go* to Edinburgh next week. (future time)
✓ They *have gone* to Edinburgh already. (past time)

WORKING IN PAIRS

Read each of the following sentences. Write down the verb and whether it is in the present, past, or future tense.

1   Morris is eating all the ice-cream.

2   I have just finished my maths homework.

3   Prakesh had sold all his books by ten o'clock.

4   Mark will visit Greece during the holidays.

5   Dad was unwilling to let Sarah stay out until 11.00.

6   Joe is going to come to London by Concorde.

7   We were planning a surprise party for my brother.

8   Sam has prepared all the food.

9   I am ready to help you with your physics.

10   You must go as soon as you are ready.

WORKING IN PAIRS

Rewrite the sentences above, changing them into any different tense by changing parts of the verb.

✓ Morris *had eaten* all the ice-cream.
✓ Morris *will have eaten* all the ice-cream.

Compare your work with another pair's work.

SUBJECT AND PREDICATE

Every sentence must have a *subject* and a *predicate*.

The *subject* is what the sentence is about. It is usually a *noun* or a *pronoun*.

> ✓ girl, teacher, sky, food, I, she, you, they

Subjects usually come at the beginning of the sentence.

> ✓ *The girl* takes violin lessons.
> ✓ *She* hates having to practise.

Subjects have one main *noun* or *pronoun* and often words describing the subject as well.

> ✓ *The tall, red-haired girl next-door* takes violin lessons.
> ✓ *The new young chemistry teacher* really knows how to teach his subject.

*EXERCISE FOR GROUP WORK

This exercise can be found on Worksheet 3.

*WORKING IN PAIRS

This exercise can be found on Worksheet 3.

The *predicate* tells what the *subject* is doing or what happens to the *subject*.

> ✓ Two boy scouts <u>tidied up our whole garden.</u>
> ✓ The teacher <u>recorded our discussion about dinosaurs.</u>
> ✓ Our cat <u>was run over by the milkman.</u>

The *predicate* is underlined.

WORKING IN PAIRS

Make up predicates *to go with the* subjects *provided below.*

Mr Sparks, the electrician,	A term of hard work
A sudden earthquake	The new dinner lady
Our new Ford Escort	A very large daddy-long-legs
A feeling of contentment	The old oak in the school playground
An old Victorian bedstead	

The *predicate* contains the *verb*. The *verb* can be one word or several words.

The *verb* is the most important part of the sentence.

WORKING IN PAIRS

Here are some subjects and predicates, but the verb is missing. Choose a verb from the list below and complete each sentence.

SUBJECTS	PREDICATES
The waves	against the sea wall.
Flies	all over the jam tart.
The bus driver	for the little old lady.
The caravan park	a fun fair and swimming pool.
Alfonso, the waiter	hot soup on the lady's lap.
My Aunt Lisa	Victorian teacups for years.
Our cricket score	325 this year.

VERBS

must have spilled	have been crawling
will provide	might exceed
ought to wait	were crashing
had been collecting	

WEAK WORDS

Any sentence can be weakened by starting it with a *weak word*.

Get to recognise the words that weaken a sentence:

after	although	as	as if
because	before	even though	if
since	that	until	

If any one of these words is placed before a sentence, the sentence becomes weak and cannot be a *strong* sentence.

> strong sentence: The cat next door attacked our dog.
> weak sentence: *Before* the cat next door attacked our dog,

*WORKING IN PAIRS 1

This exercise can be found on Worksheet 4.

WORKING IN PAIRS 2

Now that you have weakened the sentences in the exercise above (Worksheet 4), write a strong sentence for the weak sentence to lean on. Sentence 1 has been done for you. When you have finished compare your sentences with another pair's.

1   Because the kite was taller than the boy, his father had to help him fly it.

WH- WORDS

Other words that can weaken a sentence are called *wh- words*. Learn to recognise these words as well.

what	when	which	why
who	whenever	whichever	whose
where	while	whom	

 ✓ All the children waved at the helicopter <u>which flew low over the playground</u>.

 ✓ The headmaster <u>who rushed out to look too</u> also waved.

 ✓ The pilot <u>whose son attended our school</u> waved back.

The underlined weak sentences each begin with a weak word. The other words together make a strong sentence. The weak sentence leans on the strong sentence for full meaning. The weak sentence is often tucked away in the middle of the strong sentence. The weak sentence is always close to the word it describes.

*WORKING IN PAIRS 1

This exercise can be found on Worksheet 5.

WORKING IN PAIRS 2

Exercise 1

Agree on and then copy out the strong sentences from the previous exercise (Worksheet 5).
Do not include the weak sentences.

Exercise 2

Make up and write down five strong sentences. Then write five weak sentences, beginning with a wh- word. Fit the weak sentences into the strong sentences. Pass your paper to another pair so that they can judge whether your sentences are good.

Note: Exercises marked with an asterisk may be photocopied. They are to be found on the copyright-free worksheets at the end of the book.

RULE 1

Use the correct punctuation mark at the end of a sentence.

a.   **Use a full stop at the end of a sentence that tells you something.**

     ✓   Kevin tried out for the under-13s football squad.
     ✓   Some astronomers believe the universe began with a big bang.

b.   **Use a question mark at the end of a sentence that asks a question.**

     ✓   Which pupils have signed up for the debating team?
     ✓   Are you going to watch your video tonight?

     Don't use a question mark unless there really is a question asked.

     ✗   He asked if I could tell him the way home?
     ✓   He asked if I could tell him the way home.
     ✓   Is this the way home?

c.   **Use an exclamation mark after a word or sentence that shows a strong feeling.**

     ✓   Ouch! That stupid mouse has bitten me!

This exercise can be found on Worksheet 6.

RULE 2

Use commas to divide parts of a sentence into clear segments.

a. **Use commas between lists of words.**

> ✓ He gave his little sister a big, pink, fluffy, stuffed rabbit.
> ✓ Clare checked her pencil case for a pen, pencil, rubber, ruler and Tipp-Ex.

b. **Use a comma (or two) when someone is being spoken to.**

> ✓ What time does cricket practice begin, Ben?
> ✓ I still can't understand, Neeta, why you were late.

c. **Use a comma (or two) to separate spoken words from unspoken words.**

> ✓ "You will do this exercise working in groups," said the teacher.
> ✓ "And you can," she said, "begin right now."

*WORKING IN GROUPS

This exercise can be found on Worksheet 7.

d. **Use commas around a group of words that give more information about another word.**

> ✓ Mr Jones, who kept my football, wouldn't let me get it from his garden.
> ✓ My mother, hearing me shout, came running.
> ✓ Mr Khan, our maths teacher, has a lot of patience.

*WORKING IN PAIRS 1

This exercise can be found on Worksheet 8.

e. **Use a comma between two long sentences joined by 'and' or 'but'.**

✓ My granny beat everyone at table-tennis last weekend, but I beat her easily at badminton.

f. **Use a comma between two sentences joined together if the first sentence is weak.** (See page 6)

✓ Whenever my father takes me to the British Museum, we always go to see the Sutton Hoo Treasures.

✓ After I had waited for Prakesh for 35 minutes, my sister said he was going to meet me at the theatre.

g. **Use a comma to avoid confusing the reader.**

confusing: Behind the tall skyscraper rose elegantly above the squalor of the slums.

better: Behind, the tall skyscraper rose elegantly above the squalor of the slums.

*WORKING IN PAIRS 2

This exercise can be found on Worksheet 9.

RULE 3

Use a semi-colon to join strong sentences which are close in thought.

✓ I wish we had started earlier; we have missed the train.

✓ The summer was a real disappointment this year; the sun scarcely came out at all.

*WORKING IN PAIRS

This exercise can be found on Worksheet 10.

RULE 4

Use a colon to show that a list or explanation will follow.

    ✓   I love any TV programme: soap operas, sports, educational.
    ✓   I'm always late for school: getting up before 8.00 is an
          impossibility for me.

*WORKING IN PAIRS

This exercise can be found on Worksheet 11.

RULE 5

Use an apostrophe to show possession or the omission of letters.

a.   **Use an apostrophe followed by s ('s) to show possession on
          any noun that doesn't end with an s.**

    ✓   The teacher's register is on the desk.
    ✓   The children's names have all been written in.

b.   **Use an apostrophe alone to show possession, on any noun
          ending with s.**

    ✓   I left James' coat on the bench in the park.
    ✓   The boys' bicycles were all chained together.

c.   **Use an apostrophe to show that letters have been left out.**

    ✓   I don't want to start my homework yet.
    ✓   Joey could've come to the party on Friday.

Do not use apostrophes in the wrong place.

  ✗   I do'nt like this pen and I wo'nt use it.

  ✓   I don't like this pen and I won't use it.

*WORKING IN PAIRS

This exercise can be found on Worksheet 12.

RULE 6

Use a hyphen to divide words or join words

a.   **Put a hyphen at the end of a line, between syllables.**

  ✓   The game between Hampshire and Middlesex was very ex-citing.

  ✓   As we're at Baker Street, let's see whether the Planet-arium is open.

b.   **Put a hyphen when you join words, or join prefixes and words.**

  ✓   He has a lot of self-confidence.

  ✓   Granny is the only trendy seventy-five-year-old I know.

  ✓   My brother is very easy-going.

  ✓   Her ex-husband was a ne'er-do-well.

*WORKING IN PAIRS

This exercise can be found on Worksheet 13.

RULE 7

Use a dash or brackets to add unexpected information to a sentence.

  ✓   Handel (1685–1759) lived in England for about 50 years.

  ✓   I'll meet you tonight at eight o' clock — if I can get out.

*WORKING IN PAIRS

This exercise can be found on Worksheet 14.

RULE 8

Use speech marks correctly with other punctuation marks.

a. **Put speech marks around only the spoken words.**

✗ "I'd love to go on the dodgems he said."
✓ "I'd love to go on the dodgems," he said.

b. **Use a capital letter to begin the spoken words.**

✓ David shouted, "The last one in is a water rat!"

c. **Separate the spoken words from the unspoken words with a comma.**

✗ "My bedroom's a right old mess" she said.
✓ "My bedroom's a right old mess," she said.
or: "My bedroom," she said, "is a right old mess."

d. **Use a new paragraph for each new speaker.**

✓ "We've got on the wrong train, again," said Ben. "We're always doing this. We'll be late."

"It's not my fault," I said. "I told you to look at the timetable."

"Oh, they're always changing the times of the trains," he replied.

"Excuses, excuses," his sister mumbled.

e. **Put end punctuation inside the speech marks.**

✗ Nita asked, "Are you going to the Divali party"?
✓ Nita asked, "Are you going to the Divali party?"

f.   **Do not overuse speech marks.**

    ✗   "Jason has joined our class." "I hope you will make him welcome," the teacher said.

    ✓   "Jason has joined our class. I hope you will make him welcome," the teacher said.

*WORKING IN PAIRS

This exercise can be found on Worksheet 15.

RULE 9

Use capital letters to show an important word.

a.   **Use a capital letter to begin a sentence.**

    ✓   It would be great if we won the ashes.

b.   **Use a capital letter at the beginning of spoken material.**

    ✓   Marie said, "This is the last time I'm baby-sitting.

c.   **Use a capital letter to begin important names of people, places and things.**

    ✓   De Tocqueville wrote about the American Revolution in French.

d.   **Always use a capital "I" when talking about yourself.**

    ✗   Mr Clark said i was the best speller in the class.

    ✓   Mr Clark said I was the best speller in the class.

e.   **Use a capital letter to begin the first and important words in titles.**

    ✓   I really enjoyed *The Last of the Mohicans*.

f.   Do not use a capital letter for the names of seasons or directions.

> unnecessary capitals: He travelled South in Spring.
>   better: He travelled south in spring.

*GROUP EXERCISE WORK

This exercise can be found on Worksheet 15.

Note: Exercises marked with an asterisk may be photocopied. They are to be found on the copyright-free worksheets at the end of the book.

A, AN

Use *an* before a word beginning with a vowel; use *a* before all other words.

    ✓   There's nothing I like better than *an* orange.
    ✓   *A* cricket ball suddenly landed in the garden.

AFFECT, EFFECT

Affect means to cause a change

    ✓   Smoking *affects* your health.

Effect means a result.

    ✓   The *effect* of a nuclear war would be horrible.

17

*WORK THESE THROUGH

This exercise can be found on Worksheet 17.

A LOT

This should always be written as two words.

    ✓ I'd like to earn *a lot* of money in my future career.

AMONG, see BETWEEN

AMOUNT, NUMBER

Amount means a mass of material.

    ✓ A large *amount* of rubble was left on the pavement.

Number means many individual pieces.

    ✓ A great *number* of bricks were left on the pavement.

*WORK THESE THROUGH

This exercise can be found on Worksheet 18.

AN, see A

AND

Don't join too many sentences with *and*. It becomes boring.

> boring: We can all get together and we can buy Red Rover tickets and then we can go to London and see the new exhibition at the Geology Museum and when we've finished we can go to the Science Museum.

> better: After we meet, we can buy a Day Return ticket, go to London, see the exhibition at the Geology Museum, and finish up with the Science Museum.

WORK THIS THROUGH

Rewrite the following boring paragraph in a more interesting way.

She gathered together all her favourite books and then she decided to put them in different piles and she put the adventure stories in one pile and the mystery stories in another and the historical stories in another pile and then arranged them on a shelf that was balanced on the head of her bed and she hoped they would not fall on her head in the night.

BETWEEN, AMONG

Between refers to two things.

> ✓ Share these sweets *between* you and your brother.

Among refers to more than two things

> ✓ There were only seven pens *among* the thirty pupils.

*WORK THESE THROUGH

This exercise can be found on Worksheet 19.

BETWEEN YOU AND I †

The correct expression is *between you and me.*

> ✗   Let's keep this between you and I.
> ✓   Let's keep this *between you and me.*

BREATH, BREATHE

A *breath* is the actual bit of air taken into or pushed out of the lungs.

> ✓   He took a deep *breath* and held it.

Breathe is the action of taking in air and letting it out.

> ✓   She *breathed* heavily as she ran around the track.

*WORK THESE THROUGH

This exercise can be found on Worksheet 20.

CONTACT

This is an over-used word that more precisely means ring, write, or talk with.

> vague: I'll *contact* you in the morning.
> better: I'll *ring* you in the morning.

---

† Indicates incorrect usage.

WORK THESE THROUGH

Rewrite each sentence more precisely by replacing the underlined word with a more exact one.

1   He <u>contacted</u> me about the bicycle.

2   I will <u>contact</u> him when I know the date of the meeting.

3   The principal wants to <u>contact</u> the pupils who saw the accident.

4   Sejal <u>contacted</u> her cousin about the wedding.

5   The travel agent tried to <u>contact</u> you about the holiday.

CONTINUAL, CONTINUOUS

Continual means regular and frequent.

    ✓   The *continual* nagging of the scout master angered the patrol leader.

Continuous means connected, without a break.

    ✓   The *continuous* hum of the air-conditioner annoyed him.

*WORK THESE THROUGH

This exercise can be found on Worksheet 21.

COULD OF, WOULD OF, MIGHT OF, SHOULD OF, MUST OF†

These are *not* standard English. They actually mean *could have, would have, might have, should have, must have.*

    ✗   I should of known he'd disappear.
    ✓   I *should have* known he'd disappear.

† Indicates incorrect usage.

WORK THESE THROUGH

Write the following sentences in full.

1   I should of known he would be late.

2   Charles could of lent you the fare.

3   Ho Lung would of come to the party if he had been asked.

4   I might of been responsible for the broken window.

5   Mr Burke says you should of told your parents.

6   You must of known you had to bring the bus-fare.

DONE

Never use this word alone to show past time; it must be used with *have*, *has*, or *had*.

     ✗   I done it myself; he done nothing to help.
     ✓   I *have done* it myself; he *has done* nothing to help.

DON'T, DOESN'T

These words must be used with the correct subject.

     ✓   I (you, we, they) *don't* understand the problem.
but
     ✓   He (she, it) *doesn't* understand it either.

Note: Put the apostrophe in the right place.

     ✗   I do'nt remember you at all.
     ✓   I *don't* remember you at all.

WORK THESE THROUGH

Write out the sentences with the correct word.

1   The manager doesn't/don't want any more help.

2   Mr Casey doesn't/don't drink any more.

3   They doesn't/don't ever need help with physics.

4   Mina doesn't/don't understand French very well.

5   The teachers doesn't/don't make the subject clear.

6   It don't/doesn't know how to find its way home.

7   I doesn't/don't know how long the film is.

8   It doesn't/don't make any sense to me at all.

9   Sanjay don't/doesn't like tennis as much as he used to.

DUE TO, OWING TO

These phrases are over-used and ugly in compositions. Use *because of* or *because* instead.

    clumsy: He was sad owing to his mother's death.
    better: He was sad *because of* his mother's death.

    clumsy: He played badly due to not practising.
    better: He played badly *because* he hadn't practised.

WORK THESE THROUGH

Rewrite the following sentences, using because of *or* because.

1   I was late owing to my bike having a flat tyre.

2   Mrs Murphy sold her car due to the expense of running it.

3   We ordered chocolate chip ice-cream owing to there being no raspberry ripple.

4   There were few apples on the trees due to the dry summer.

5   Meeta threw away the samosas owing to their age.

6   Helen liked Peter a lot due to his cute smile and curly hair.

7   I must go straight home due to the late hour.

EFFECT, see AFFECT, EFFECT

EITHER . . . OR, NEITHER . . . NOR

These words are often used in pairs. Always use them between parts of the sentence that look similar.

> poor: We can either go to a cinema or a disco.
> better: We can go *either* <u>to a cinema</u> *or* <u>to a disco</u>.

> poor: He likes neither spinach nor will he eat any kind of beans.
> better: He likes *neither* <u>spinach</u> *nor* <u>beans</u>.

(Parts of the sentence that are similar are underlined.)

WORK THESE THROUGH

One of the following sentences is written correctly. Find the correct one then correct and rewrite the other four sentences. Underline the parts of the sentence on your copy that are similar and joined by either . . . or *or* neither . . . nor.

1   You can come home either with me or go with Mark.

2   Jeff can understand neither physics nor does chemistry mean anything to him.

3   You must either ring your mother or send a message home with your sister.

4   The hardware shop can neither cut a key nor will they tell me how to get the locker open.

5   Either we can go by bus to Edinburgh or by train.

EXCEPT, EXPECT

The spelling of these two words is often confused. The use of them is quite different.

> ✓ I *expect* he will attend school as soon as he's well.
> ✓ Everyone wanted to be in the play *except* Kate and me.

FARTHER, FURTHER

Farther means a place at a distance.

> ✓ The house is *farther* than I thought.

Further means more, additional.

> ✓ We can ring and ask for *further* information.

*WORK THESE THROUGH

This exercise can be found on Worksheet 22.

FEWER, LESS

Fewer means a smaller number of individual items.

> ✓ *Fewer* visitors came than we had hoped for.

Less means a smaller amount of something.

> ✓ You must eat *less* sugar or you'll get fat.

*WORK THESE THROUGH

This exercise can be found in Worksheet 23.

FURTHER, see FARTHER, FURTHER

HARDLY, SCARCELY

These words have a negative meaning and should not be used in a sentence with *no* or *not*.

      ✗   I don't know hardly anyone here.
      ✓   I know *hardly* anyone here.
or   I know *scarcely* anyone here.

*WORK THESE THROUGH

This exercise can be found on Worksheet 24.

HIM, HER AND ME

These words should not be used as part of the subject of a sentence where *he*, *she*, or *I* must be used. Usually something is done to or for *him*, *her* and *me*.

      ✗   Him and me agreed to clean the bathroom.
      ✓   *He and I* agreed to clean the bathroom.
or   Mother asked *him and me* to clean the bathroom.

WORK THESE THROUGH

Five of the following sentences use him, her *and* me *correctly. Four are incorrect. Tick the correct sentences. Rewrite the wrong ones so that they are correct.*

1   Jody called to him and me from the attic window.

2   Her and me went to France with Mum.

3   Leroy and me annoyed Mr Tobias by cutting and selling all the daffodils in the park.

4　　　　The school gave her and me a prize each.

5　　　　Jan and me often get smacked by Dad for answering back.

6　　　　The sweets were shared between him and her.

7　　　　Uncle Joe bought leather jackets for Bart and me.

8　　　　I'm sure that Ol will lend him and her five pounds.

9　　　　Mayur and me were refused permission to ride to school by the principal.

HIMSELF, see MYSELF, etc

HISSELF, THEIRSELVES †

These words are *not* acceptable usage. Use *himself* or *themselves* instead.

　　✗　He told me the story hisself.
　　✓　He told me the story *himself.*

　　✗　They arranged the trip theirselves.
　　✓　They arranged the trip *themselves.*

IMPLY, INFER

To imply is to suggest an idea without saying it.

　　✓　John's answer *implies* he has read the book, even though he hasn't.

To infer is to draw a meaning from something.

　　✓　I *infer* that he hates the course from the way he behaves.

The speaker or writer *implies* things; the listener or reader *infers* things.

† Indicates incorrect usage.

*WORK THESE THROUGH

This exercise can be found on Worksheet 25.

ITS, IT'S

Its is used to show ownership or possession.

> ✓ The dog ran after *its* own tail.

It's means 'it is'.

> ✓ *It's* a long time since we've had a sunny day.

*WORK THESE THROUGH

This exercise can be found on Worksheet 26.

KNEW, NEW

Knew is the past tense of *know*.

> ✓ I *knew* you would ring.

New is something that is not old.

> ✓ My shoes are brand *new*.

LATER, LATTER

These words are often confused in spelling. They have clearly separate meanings.

Later means some time after now.

> ✓ I will see you *later* this afternoon.

Latter means nearer the end.

> ✓ He spent the *latter* part of the week preparing for the exam.

LAYING, see LYING, LAYING

LEAD, LED (words that rhyme with *bed*)

Led is the past tense for the verb *lead* (rhymes with *seed*)

> ✓ Montgomery *led* his troops into battle in World War Two.

Lead is a metal.

> ✓ These old toy soldiers are made of *lead*.

WORK THESE THROUGH

Write out the sentences with the correct word in each sentence.

1 Often there is lead/led in old paintwork.

2 The path lead/led across an open field.

3 My brother is frequently lead/led astray by wild friends.

4 We have a toy that makes lead/led soldiers by melting down old pieces of lead/led.

5 My grandfather has lead/led a fascinating life.

6 He lead/led a company of soldiers in the last war.

7 Thieves sometimes steal the lead/led off church roofs.

8 Mr Morris lead/led the crocodile of pupils across the road.

9 Daddy hit the burglar with a lead/led pipe.

LESS, see FEWER, LESS

LOSE, LOOSE

Lose means to fail to find.

> ✓   I *lose* my pen about six times a day.

Loose means not tight.

> ✓   You cannot hang a man with a *loose* noose.

*WORK THESE THROUGH

This exercise can be found on Worksheet 27.

LYING, LAYING

Lying means resting, as on a bed.

> ✓   Kevin is ill and is *lying* down for a while.

Laying means placing or putting down.

> ✓   My mother was *laying* my football clothes on the table.

*WORK THESE THROUGH

This exercise can be found on Worksheet 28.

ME, see HIM, HER AND ME

MIGHT OF†, see COULD OF†

MUST OF,† see COULD OF†

MYSELF, HIMSELF, HERSELF, ITSELF, YOURSELF, THEMSELVES

a. **These words are used to make the words *I*, *he*, *she*, *it*, *you*, *they* stronger.**

✓ *I myself* offered to take her to the party.

b. **These words come after the verb and refer to person(s) already mentioned.**

✓ *He* asked *himself* why he had taken the money.

c. **These words should not be used when *I*, *me*, *him*, *her*, *you*, *them* would be more straightforward.**

weak: The teacher laughed at John and myself.
better: The teacher laughed at *John and me*.

weak: Prakesh and myself were studying together.
better: *Prakesh* and I were studying together.

*WORK THESE THROUGH

This exercise can be found on Worksheet 29.

† Indicates incorrect usage.

WORK THESE THROUGH

Rewrite the following sentences correctly.

1   Roger and myself will prepare dinner.

2   The bakery offered Nita and myself a job.

3   I want to send Ranji and yourself to Kodak for training.

NEW, see KNEW

NEITHER . . . NOR, see EITHER . . . OR

NOT ONLY . . . BUT ALSO

These words are often used in pairs. Always use them between parts of the sentence that look similar.

> poor: Borg not only was a good athlete but also he was a
>   gentlemanly sportsman.
> better: Borg was *not only* a good athlete *but also* a gentlemanly
>   sportsman.

(Parts of the sentence that are similar are underlined.)

WORK THESE THROUGH

One of the following sentences is written correctly. Correct and rewrite the other three sentences. On your copy underline the similar parts of the sentence that are joined by not only . . . but also.

1   We want not only to succeed but also we want to be the best.

2   Margy is not only clever but also is a very courteous class member.

3   The Patels not only invited us over but also wanted to hear about our trip to India.

4   You can win not only a trip to New York but also you get a new wardrobe worth five hundred pounds.

NUMBER, see AMOUNT, NUMBER

OFF, OF

Off means to change a place or position.

    ✓   He got *off* the table when I entered.

Of means belonging to

    ✓   This is one *of* my best friends.

*WORK THESE THROUGH

This exercise can be found on Worksheet 30.

ONLY

Only means *and nothing more.* It should be placed next to the word it is limiting.

    vague: He only eats peanut butter.
                (meaning: He doesn't polish his shoes or do anything else with peanut butter.)
    better: He eats only peanut butter.
                (meaning: He doesn't eat anything else.)

WORK THESE THROUGH

The word only *is in the wrong place. Rewrite the sentences, putting it in a more appropriate place.*

1   The bank clerk only gave me twenty pounds.

2   Marie only paid her share of the bill.

3   I only drank one cup of water.

4   Benjamin only agreed to baby-sit on Friday evening.

5   Melissa only wrote her mother two letters over the summer.

6   The drunk driver only hurt himself in the car crash; the others were uninjured.

7   Shezad only finished the written part of the exam.

8   Our neighbours only plant red flowers in their garden.

9   The school teachers only voted for one of the prefects.

OWING TO, see DUE TO

PASSED, PAST

Passed means actual moving, performing an action.

    ✓   With eyes down Sandra *passed* the teacher.
    ✓   I have *passed* my maths exam at long last.

Past means a time gone by or somewhere beyond.

    ✓   Old people tend to live in the *past*.
    ✓   My ex-boyfriend stared *past* me.

*WORK THESE THROUGH

This exercise can be found on worksheet 31.

PRACTICE, PRACTISE

a.   ***Practice* means a skill, custom, repeated work.**

    ✓   It's the *practice* of British Rail to fine fare-dodgers.

b.   ***Practise* means to perform an action.**

    ✓   You can *practise* tonight after supper.

*WORK THESE THROUGH

This exercise can be found on Worksheet 32.

PRINCIPAL, PRINCIPLE

Principal means first in rank or something which is most important.

    ✓   My *principal* reason for studying is to get good GCSEs.

Principle means a rule or truth.

    ✓   Politicians should live by honest *principles*.

WORK THESE THROUGH

Write out the correct word for the sentence.

1   I have one principal/principle: never lend money.

2   Every government sets up principals/principles to rule by.

3   The principal/principle has called a meeting for 3.00 p.m.

4   The principal/principle food of many children is fish and chips.

5   I find it difficult to live up to your principles/principals.

6   The principal/principle cause of the disaster was lack of rainfall.

7   His problem is that he has money and ability, but no
         principals/principles.

8   My brother's principal/principle problem is that he prefers cricket to
         physics.

QUIET, QUITE

Quiet means with little noise, calm.

    ✓   E.T. came from outer space where it's *quiet*.

Quite means rather or completely.

    ✓   This room gets *quite* warm when the heater is on.
    ✓   I am *quite* content at the moment.

*WORK THESE THROUGH

This exercise can be found on Worksheet 33.

SCARCELY, see HARDLY, SCARCELY

SHOULD OF†, see COULD OF†

---

†Indicates incorrect usage.

SO, VERY

These words are often used as if they were the same, but *so* should be used with *that*.

weak:	The teacher was so angry.
better:	The teacher was *so angry that* everyone was frightened.
or:	The teacher was *very* angry.

THAN, THEN

Than is used when comparing two things.

> ✓ He is taller *than* his father.

Then means at a particular time.

> ✓ *Then* we all walked into the room together.

*WORK THESE THROUGH

This exercise can be found on Worksheet 34.

THAT, see WHO

THEIR, THERE, THEY'RE

Their shows ownership.

> ✓ My parents were pleased *their* car wasn't damaged.

There is used to indicate a place or to start a sentence.

> ✓   Mother goes *there* to her weight-watchers club.
> ✓   *There* was a long low moan from the cupboard.

They're means they are.

> ✓   My friends say *they're* coming for a visit in July.

*WORK THESE THROUGH

This exercise can be found on Worksheet 35.

THEIRSELVES †, see HISSELF, THEIRSELVES †

THEM THINGS †, (them people, them vegetables, etc.)

This is *not* standard usage. Use 'these' or 'those'.

> ✗   I hated them kids as soon as they came in.
> ✓   I hated *those* kids as soon as they came in.

THEMSELVES, see MYSELF

THEN, see THAN

---

† Indicates incorrect usage.

THROUGH, THOROUGH

These words are often confused in spelling but the meanings are quite different.

Through means in at one end or side and out at the other.

> ✓ He walked *through* the room.

Thorough means complete in every way.

> ✓ He made a *thorough* study of dinosaurs.
> ✓ I made a *thorough* fool of myself.

TO, TOO, TWO

To often shows direction.

> ✓ He walks *to* school with his brother.

Too means *also* or *a great amount.*

> ✓ I invited Ranjeet, *too*.
> ✓ There is *too* much butter on this bread.

Two is the number 2.

> ✓ Buy *two* tickets: one for you and one for Mike.

WORK THESE THROUGH

Write out the sentences with the correct forms of the word.

1   This train is just to/too slow.

2   I had to/too much pudding for dinner.

3   The boy was taken to/too hospital.

4   Jason reported the theft to/too the headmaster.

5   The children will go to/too if they are invited.

6   My sister feels to/too ill to come to school.

7   Sanjay went to/too school much to/too early.

8   The violinist wouldn't perform because the audience was to/too noisy.

9   I think I'll write to/too your too/two cousins to/too.

WEATHER, WHETHER

These words are very often misspelled. There are only the two ways above of spelling them. Their meanings are very different.

Weather is the climate.

Whether means one way or another and is often used with *not*.

> ✓   I don't know *whether* I like it or not.
> ✓   He will say later *whether* he's coming or not.

WHERE, WERE

Where means a place or direction.

> ✓   I know *where* he lives.

Were is the past of *are*.

> ✓   We *were* all glad to see him.

*WORK THESE THROUGH

This exercise can be found on Worksheet 36.

WHO, WHICH, THAT

Who refers to people.

    ✓   I'll ring Mrs Smith *who* is our baby-sitter.

Which refers to animals or things.

    ✓   These are the tropical fish *which* eat so much.

That refers to people, animals or things.

    ✓   I lost the ring *that* you gave me.
    ✓   I don't know the man *that* you're talking about.

*WORK THESE THROUGH

This exercise can be found on Worksheet 37.

WHOSE, WHO'S

a.   **Whose shows possession or ownership.**

    ✓   *Whose* books are on the table?

b.   **Who's means who is or who has.**

    ✓   *Who's* going to the cinema with us?
    ✓   I don't know *who's* borrowed my plimsolls.

*WORK THESE THROUGH

This exercise can be found on Worksheet 38.

WOULD OF†, see COULD OF†

YOUR, YOU'RE

Your shows possession.

    ✓   I'm sure these are *your* books.

You're means 'you are'.

    ✓   *You're* the first person on my list of invitations.

*WORK THESE THROUGH

This exercise can be found on Worksheet 39.

---

†Indicates incorrect usage.

YOURSELF, see **MYSELF**

Note: Exercises marked with an asterisk may be photocopied. They are to be found on the copyright-free worksheets at the end of the book.

RULE 1

Write 'will' or 'would' in 'If'–sentences.

a.   **'If'-sentences that show what is *possible* should use the *present tense* in the *if* half of the sentence and *will* in the other half of the sentence.**

     ✓   If we *go* to the swimming bath now, we *will* have three hours of swimming.

     ✓   If you *eat* all the cake at lunch, there *will* be none for tea.

b.   **'If'-sentences that show what is *unlikely* should use the *past tense* in the *if* half of the sentence and *would* in the other half of the sentence.**

     ✓   If a burglar *broke* into my house, I *would* hide under the bed.

     ✓   If you *joined* the sea-scouts, you *would* learn how to sail.

*GROUP EXERCISE WORK

This exercise can be found on Worksheet 40.

GROUP EXERCISE WORK

Working with a partner write five 'If-sentences' to show what is possible. You are given suggestions in the brackets.

> (write exam paper, A)
> ✓ If Adam *writes* a good exam paper, he *will* get an A.

1 (babysit, money)

2 (tidy desk, happy)

3 (like pop-music, my new record)

4 (sleepy, fretful)

5 (like reading, *The Secret Diary of Adrian Mole*)

In the next group of sentences, use the clues to show what is unlikely.

> (save, rich)
> ✓ If I *saved* my money, I *would* be rich.

1 (watch TV, homework)

2 (America, by boat)

3 (win competition, car)

4 (break window, run)

5 (practise, soloist)

RULE 2

Change pronouns and verbs when reporting speech.

When reporting what someone else said at an earlier time, it is necessary to change pronouns, verbs and sometimes other words.

> quoted speech: "*I love* playing cards," she said.
> reported speech: She said *she loved* playing cards.

| quoted speech: | *"Tomorrow, we will* go to Madame Tussaud's," he said. |
| reported speech: | He said that *they would* go to Madame Tussaud's *the next day*. |

The changes in the verb usually follow this pattern:

is	becomes	was
can	becomes	could
has/have	becomes	had
may	becomes	might
will	becomes	would
likes	becomes	like*d*
tell	becomes	told
like*d*	becomes	*had* like*d*
told	becomes	had told

GROUP EXERCISE WORK

Change the underlined words in the following sentences, writing the sentences out in reported speech.

| quoted speech: | "I like your new album," he said. |
| reported speech: | He said he liked my new album. |

1   "I can understand your problem," he said.

2   "We may not arrive in time for tea," she said.

3   "I will return your book when I have finished it," she said.

4   "We have bought tickets for the concert," Mary said.

5   "Joe has borrowed your plimsolls for the game tomorrow," I told Eddie.

6   "Margot owes me this money," Sam said.

7   His aunt told him, "I will see you after school."

8   "Will you please phone as soon as you get home?" Granny asked them.

9   "Tomorrow I will leave for my holiday in Italy," she said.

RULE 3

Put an -s on the present tense of a verb, if the subject is 'he', 'she', or 'it', or a word that could replace 'he', 'she', or 'it'.

    ✗   She usually get high marks on her work.
    ✓   She usually *gets* high marks on her work.

    ✗   John practise football every afternoon.
    ✓   John *practises* football every afternoon.

*GROUP EXERCISE WORK

This exercise can be found on Worksheet 41.

RULE 4

If you begin in one tense, stay in it. Don't keep changing.

    ✗   Out I go to the bicycle shed and find my bike was gone.
    ✓   Out I *went* to the bicycle shed and *found* my bike *was gone*.
  or: Out I *go* to the bicycle shed and *find* my bike *is gone*.

    ✗   So he walks up to his best friend and asked for a pound.
    ✓   So he *walked* up to his best friend and *asked* for a pound.
  or: So he *walks* up to his best friend and *asks* for a pound.

Note: Skilled writers sometimes change tenses in the middle of a story, but you should stick to one tense unless you have a good reason not to.

GROUP EXERCISE WORK

An article appeared in the local paper about children being rude on buses. A pupil from the school wrote an answer to the article. Rewrite the letter, correcting the tense mistakes only where necessary.

Dear Sir,

Yesterday I was standing at the bus stop waiting for the bus to take me to school when my bus pulls up. It is almost empty, but as soon as all the adults get on, the driver pulls away. I was very upset because, what happens is that I arrive late for school.

On my way home, two buses passed by and didn't stop. When we are able to get on a bus, the conductor talks to us as if we are hoodlums and threatens to put us off the bus. We were not misbehaving at all.

It isn't fair to treat school-children so rudely. We were not brought up badly. Something ought to have been done about people being rude to school-children.

Yours faithfully,

James Young.

RULE 5

Use the correct form when you compare people or things.

a.   **If you compare two people or things put -er on short words.**

   ✓   Marie is *taller* than her sister.
   ✓   Nevertheless, her sister is *prettier* than she is.

However, add *more* to long words.

   ✓   John's father is a *more careful* driver than my dad.
   ✓   Keith is *more determined* to join the team than I am.

Never use *more* with a describing word that ends in -er.

   ✗   I am feeling more better today.
   ✓   I am feeling *better* today.

b. **When comparing three or more people or things, use -est on short words.**

> ✓ This is the *hardest* problem in the whole exercise.
> ✓ Tim is the *kindest* boy in the whole class.

Use *most* with longer words.

> ✓ This is the *most depressing* day I've ever had.
> ✓ Fiver was the *most mysterious* rabbit in the novel.

Never use *most* with a describing word that ends in -*est*.

> ✗ It was the most happiest moment of my life.
> ✓ It was the *happiest* moment of my life.

*GROUP EXERCISE WORK

This exercise can be found on Worksheet 42.

RULE 6

When using a pronoun to refer to another word, make clear which word you are referring to.

a. **Don't switch from a general word to 'you'.**

> clumsy: If a person doesn't do the homework, the teacher is on to you straight away.
>
> better: If *you* don't do *your* homework, the teacher is on to *you* straight away.
>
> or: If *I* don't do *my* homework the teacher is on to *me* straight away.

b. **Be sure there is a word for the pronoun to refer back to.**

> confusing: When Joe started bunking school, they rang his parents.
> (It is not clear who 'they' refers to.)

clear: When Joe started bunking school, *the school secretary* rang his parents.

c.   **Make the pronoun refer back to only one particular word.**

confusing: My cousins are coming with us for the summer holidays. They are usually good fun.
              (*They* can refer to either my cousins or the summer holidays.)

better: *My cousins* are usually good fun. *They* are coming with us for the summer holidays.

GROUP EXERCISE WORK

Re-write the following sentences so that the pronouns refer to the correct word. Between the brackets at the beginning of the sentence, write which rule you used.

1   ( ) Marie is very keen to do metalwork and electronics, but they are forcing her into needlework and cookery.

2   ( ) If a person is going to get really good at snooker, you have to practise about three hours a day.

3   ( ) Leroy says he could have been an Olympic swimmer but he's never done anything with it.

4   ( ) Henry spent all afternoon baking biscuits for the members of his youth club, but they were really horrid.

Note: Exercises marked with an asterisk may be photocopied. They are to be found on the copyright-free worksheets at the end of the book.

Here are some *suggestions* for helping you to solve your own spelling problems. Following the suggestions are four *rules*. These rules can also help your spelling, but for every rule there will always be exceptions. So use the rules to help you as much as possible and if the rule fails, practise the suggestions.

SUGGESTION 1

Make spelling a physical activity involving looking, speaking and writing.

a.   Write the word correctly.
b.   Say it aloud, pronouncing each syllable. Even pronounce silent letters if it helps, for example, climb.
c.   Close your eyes and picture the word for one minute.
d.   Trace over the word three times, saying each letter.

WORKING IN PAIRS

Below are five words that usually cause difficulty. Learn these words by following the four steps above. If you know these words, you and your partner should each pick out three words that you always get wrong and follow the same procedure.

benefited
conscious
privilege
vehicle
February

SUGGESTION 2

Circle the tricky spots of words which regularly cause problems. Then study only the few letters that go wrong.

*WORKING IN PAIRS

This exercise can be found on Worksheet 43.

SUGGESTION 3

Learn to apply the 'ie' rhymed rule. Remember it in three parts:

(1)   *i* **before** *e*
(2)   **except after** *c*
(3)   **or when pronounced other than** *ee*.

*WORKING IN PAIRS 1

This exercise can be found on Worksheet 44.

*WORKING IN PAIRS 2

This exercise can be found on Worksheet 44.

SUGGESTION 4

Make up memorable sentences for words which are real problems for you.

Use each letter to form a word. Then make a sentence of the words.

> ✓ Don't eat frogs in Neasden if the eels look yummy.
>   = *definitely*

or make up explaining sentences:

> ✓ There are a pair of *a*'s in sep*a*rate.

WORKING IN PAIRS

Working with a partner, make up either a memorable sentence or an explaining sentence for each of these words, or use any three words that either of you has trouble with.

occasion
athlete
succeed

Close your book and see if the sentence helps you remember how to spell the words.

SUGGESTION 5

Watch out for common words that cause trouble when simple endings (suffixes) are added.

Below are words that are very commonly misspelled because of suffixes.

coming	the e on come must be dropped.
hoping/hopping	look at the difference – then use the correct one: – the first is wishing for something. – the second is jumping up and down.
gorgeous	if you want to keep the soft g sound in words put an e after the g.
noticeable	if you want to keep the c as an s sound before an ending keep the e after c.
shining	this is often misspelled with two *n*'s.

Special care must be taken when you have to decide whether to double or not to double consonants before an ending. You should watch your essays to see which words you have trouble with, for example, *coming, hoping, shining,* etc. and treat them as your problem words, using Suggestions 1 and 2.

WORKING IN PAIRS

With your partner look over some of your old essays and make a list of five words that, between you, you commonly get wrong when you add an ending.

SUGGESTION 6

Here are a few easy prefix/suffix rules. Try to learn and apply one of these every two or three weeks.

Rule 1

Prefixes come at the beginning of words. Put the prefix on to the word without adding or subtracting any letters either to the original word, or to the prefix.

Prefix		Word		Respelled
dis	+	appear	=	disappear
il	+	legal	=	illegal
mis	+	take	=	mistake
un	+	necessary	=	unnecessary

WORKING IN PAIRS

In Column 1 below are prefixes. Copy the list and join each prefix to its word in Column 2; then with a partner test each other on these new words and the words in the example above.

Column 1		Column 2
im	+	moral
mis	+	spell
dis	+	satisfy
im	+	mature
dis	+	agree
un	+	natural
dis	+	please

WORKING IN PAIRS

Copy the list of words and circle the prefix; then write out the word without the prefix.

illiterate	discredit
incorrect	impolite
dissimilar	irregular
undecided	unreliable

Rule 2

When a word containing *ll* is joined to another word, *ll* becomes *l*.

bash + full	= bashful		un	+ till	= until
full + fill	= fulfil		well	+ come	= welcome
skill + full	= skilful				

WORKING IN PAIRS

Write out correctly spelled each of the following words; then check your spelling with your partner's. The first word has been done for you.

```
thank    + full    = thankful
all      + ways    =
joy      + full    =
all      + ready   =
spite    + full    =
wonder   + full    =
peace    + full    =
all      + though  =
will     + full    =
```

Rule 3

a.   ***If a consonant comes before y, change y to i and add es,***

b.   ***If a vowel comes before y, just add s.***

*WORKING IN PAIRS

This exercise can be found on Worksheet 45.

Rule 4

Endings that begin with a consonant are usually just added to a word. There is no change in the word.

```
care    + less  = careless

sincere + ly    = sincerely

govern  + ment  = government

safe    + ty    = safety
```

WORKING IN PAIRS

Copy out and divide the words below in the same way as the words are divided in the examples on page 56. Circle the consonant that starts each ending. The first word has been done for you.

arrangement   arrange + (m)ent

largely

sadness

severely

hopeless

SUGGESTION 7

Improving your spelling is your own decision.

No set of rules is going to make you instantly a brilliant speller. If *you* want to get better at spelling, keep a notebook and record all the problem words, the ones that are always being corrected in your writing.

Find out from a teacher, parent, or a classmate who is a good speller how to spell the word. Use a dictionary if you can make a good enough guess to find the word there. Then focus on the part of the word that you always get wrong. Most of the word you'll probably be able to spell.

Learn only one or two words a day; trying to learn more is boring and often confusing. There is a list on page 58 that might be a good starting place.

If you make a decision to study spelling regularly, there are many books of spelling rules to help you. One good book is:

A. M. Burt, *A Guide to Better Spelling*, Stanley Thornes (Publishers) Ltd.

CHECKLIST FOR 50 SPELLINGS

All the words used as examples in the spelling section of this book often cause problems.

Below is a list of 50 commonly misspelled words, all taken from students' papers. The problem letters in each word are in bold type. If you usually get any of these words wrong, study the bold type letters. Use Suggestions 1 and 2 especially to help you remember how to spell your problem words correctly.

across	envi**ron**ment	prob**ably**
am**ong**	**etc.**	pro**cee**d
app**ar**ent	exa**gg**erate	pur**su**e
arg**um**ent	fa**sc**inate	real**ly**
ath**le**te	h**eig**ht	reco**mm**end
ans**w**er	inter**est**	refe**rr**ing
beautiful	lon**ely**	reme**m**ber
bel**ie**ve	lo**s**ing	rhythm
breath**e**	nece**ss**ary	since**re**ly
Brit**ai**n	nin**e**ty	stub**b**orn
busin**e**ss	o**cc**asion	su**cc**eed
careful	o**cc**urred	su**pp**ose
ca**rr**ying	opinion	surprise
con**sc**ious	prec**e**de	swi**mm**ing
dining	profe**ss**ion	tomorrow
disas**tr**ous	posse**ss**ion	women
emba**rr**ass	privilege	writing

COPYRIGHT-FREE WORKSHEETS

Worksheet 1   Nouns (Page 1)

WORKING IN PAIRS

The nouns in the following paragraph are underlined. Above each one, write whether it is a person, object, place or idea.

Oliver kept his grass snake in a box in his bedroom. He named it Sam. Children came from all over the neighbourhood to play with such an unusual pet. They let it slide down their shirts, out of their sleeves, around their necks. Not one single child ever showed any fear.

CONTINUED PAIRWORK

In the next paragraph, underline all the nouns. There are 23 nouns in all. After you have completed your underlining, check your answers with another pair. Above each one, write whether it is a person, object, place or idea.

One morning Sam had disappeared from the box. Oliver rushed out of his room calling his mum and dad. The thought of having such a creature loose in the house didn't please his parents. Granny was coming to tea the following day, which added to their anxiety. Her annoyance would be clearly shown if Sam should suddenly slither up her leg. Oliver's father searched the bedroom thoroughly, and then began pulling up floorboards. No one even caught a glimpse of the escaped reptile.

Worksheet 2   Verbs (Page 3)

WORKING IN PAIRS

In the following two paragraphs, underline all the verbs. Circle all the helping verbs.

Paragraph 1

It must have been six years since he had moved into his tree-house, but he felt it might only have been yesterday. He doubted that he ever would leave, or so he had told his friends, smiling coyly at his own pun and repeating 'wood leaf'. "I am becoming a bit like the tree, itself," he had murmured softly, and one could have detected a similarity between a tree sighing in the breeze and Mr Pepper's voice. And if one were to look closely, one would notice a darkening of the colour and a roughening of the skin texture that one might not have expected in someone of Mr Pepper's age.

Paragraph 2

Alison had been hit by a car. She didn't know what was going on. She could remember quite clearly that she was skipping along – and now she was laid out on some stranger's sofa. She couldn't understand why all these strange faces were peering down at her. Mummy was crying and Daddy did look very anxious. She should be able to remember what had happened. She must have tried to cross the road without looking. She ought to have known better.

Worksheet 3 Subject and Predicate (Page 5)

EXERCISE FOR GROUP WORK

Working with a partner, join each subject with an appropriate predicate to make a whole sentence. Then compare your work with another pair's work. The first one has been done for you.

SUBJECT	PREDICATE
A sudden gust of wind	made a perfect slide.
	are glued to the TV from dawn to dusk.
Mr Quirck, the plumber,	
Adolph, my goldfish	am skilled at avoiding work.
A high bank of mud	cracked our basin, putting it in.
I	jerked the clothes off the line.
Some people	has a black patch above his eye.

WORKING IN PAIRS

Below is a list of predicates. Work together to provide a list of subjects to go with the predicates. Try to put at least three words in each subject.

SUBJECTS	PREDICATES
_____	enjoyed the day at Alton Towers.
_____	has made the pitch too wet.
_____	skidded into a wall.
_____	baked six cakes for the fair.
_____	miaowed pathetically at the door.
_____	tumbled down a flight of stairs.
_____	brought tears to Mother's eyes.
_____	looked worriedly at the envelope.

Worksheet 4   Weak Words (Page 6)

WORKING IN PAIRS

The sentences below are strong. Weaken each of them by putting one of the weak words listed on page 6 in front of each sentence. The first one has been done for you.

Change the full stop to a comma.

1. The kite was taller than the boy.
   Because the kite was taller than the boy,

2. Neil's language is very coarse.

3. Our cat got in the neighbour's flower bed.

4. The school tennis courts are waterlogged.

5. Carla's pet cockerel suddenly laid an egg.

6. Mr Temple left his hat on the bus.

7. I won the snooker trophy for the under-15s.

8. I promised to help Nicky with her maths.

9. Bert has gone on an adventure holiday.

10. Some football supporters smashed up a train.

Worksheet 5   Wh- Words (Page 7)

WORKING IN PAIRS 1

Underline the wh- weak sentences within the following strong sentences. Circle the word that begins the weak sentence.

1   Benjamin was not at the bus stop where he usually stood.

2   The coach driver who picked him up for camp looked up and down the road.

3   The road which Benjamin always walked down was completely empty.

4   Suddenly the door of the shop which sold sweets was flung open.

5   Benjamin, whose cheeks were bulging, rushed toward the waiting coach.

Worksheet 6   Rule 1 (Page 9)

WORKING IN GROUPS

The following paragraph was submitted to the school magazine. It contains some errors at the ends of sentences, but most of the punctuation is correct. Working with your group, make any corrections that you think are necessary. Above any correction you make, write the letter of the rule that you used to make the correction. Be sure you all agree.

How would you like to win a season ticket to the ABC cinema. You can do it. The ticket can be yours. It's as simple as winking. All you have to do is persuade your teacher to take her class to three of the New Classic Films we are showing over the next year. Wouldn't you like to see *Animal Farm* as a film. Pick up a leaflet now. Get your teacher to fill in the form and a free ticket is yours. Hurry. There are only ten more free tickets left.

Worksheet 7   Rule 2 (Page 10)

WORKING IN GROUPS

*The following exercise contains a few mistakes. Commas have been left out. By referring to the rules **a** to **c**, you can make any necessary corrections. Working with your group, see if you can find the mistakes. Agree on the rule you use to correct them, and write the letter of the rule above the correction. The first sentence has been done for you.*

1   I think this pen is yours,^{b} Katy.

2   Mother told you Simon to pick up your clothes.

3   He bought sweets peanuts crisps sausage rolls and fizzy drinks for the party.

4   "Will you" he asked "be able to bring a cricket bat Dan?"

5   "I'm afraid mine is broken" Dan answered.

6   "I can't lay the table if there are no knives forks spoons or glasses" he said.

7   Ranjeet you can hand out the books paper and pencils.

Worksheet 8   Rule 2 (Page 10)

WORKING IN PAIRS 1

*Working with a partner, put commas around the group of words that give added information. Match the sentences to one of the examples used under **d**. Write the number of the example which makes the closest match to each sentence. The first sentence has been done for you.*

1   Mr James, an American friend, drove the wrong way around a roundabout.   (3)

2   He seeing approaching cars got quite frightened.   (   )

3   Jamming on the brakes he skidded sideways.   (   )

4   A bobby who had been watching all this walked towards the car.   (   )

5   Mr James who had experienced the angry words of American policemen in the past felt his heart sink.   (   )

6   The bobby a huge blue-uniformed figure bent down and peered through the window.   (   )

7   Looking at Mr James with amazement he said, "We seldom see anyone do that, sir."

(adapted from The Reader's Digest)

Worksheet 9   Rule 2 (Page 11)

WORKING IN PAIRS 2

*Put in the missing commas in the following sentences. Decide which of the rules, **e**, **f**, or **g**, you have followed to make the correction. On the line, write the letter of the part of the rule you have used. When you finish see if your answers are the same as another pair's. The first sentence has been done for you.*

1   Below, the aged pier creaked and groaned as each wave struck.   _g_

2   Although I play table-tennis every day Granny still manages to beat me.   ____

3   Andrea spent all of last week going to the sales but nothing she tried on suited her.   ____

4   Because he is so lazy about getting up we are going to be late for the play.   ____

5   John spent three weeks in France this summer and his parents have arranged for him to go back there over the Christmas holiday.   ____

6   Outside the large Victorian house appeared to be in excellent condition.   ____

Worksheet 10   Rule 3 (Page 11)

WORKING IN PAIRS

Put the semi-colon in the correct place in each sentence.

1   Skiing is my favourite sport I won a gold medal in a competiition last year.

2   I hardly ever watch TV in the summer there are always so many other things to do.

3   Chris was late for school again today the bus was full by the time it got to his stop.

4   I am going to school early from now on I will then have time to play on the computers.

Worksheet 11   Rule 4 (Page 12)

WORKING IN PAIRS

In the sentences below, add a colon where it should go.

1   My brother won't do anything around the house tidy his room, help
         with the washing up, cook, even put his own shoes away.

2   Pollution now affects every aspect of our lives food, water, air, even
         our moments of quiet.

3   Football, cricket and tennis these are my favourite sports.

4   Not what you'd call hard-working a number of students are like this.

Worksheet 12   Rule 5 (Page 12)

WORKING IN PAIRS

*The apostrophes have been used correctly in the next sentences. Above each
apostrophe, write **a**, **b**, or **c**, depending on which apostrophe rule was used.
Check your answers with another pair. The first sentence has been done for you.*

1   The girls*ᵇ* bicycles were all crammed into the shelter.

2   Jason's answers are usually right, aren't they?

3   I haven't understood why Charles' appointment was cancelled.

4   We wouldn't be allowed to borrow anyone's books.

5   Julius' plimsolls weren't found in his brother's bag.

6   The card was covered with the pupils' signatures.

Worksheet 13   Rule 6 (Page 13)

WORKING IN PAIRS

The following sentences require hyphens. Put them in the correct places.

1   My seven year old brother is a real cry baby.

2   If he's not crying he's wearing a holier than thou expression.

3   Sabir spent thirty two pounds on those physics books.

4   The other half of the semi detached burned down.

Worksheet 14   Rule 7 (Page 13)

WORKING IN PAIRS

In the sentences below put in the dashes or brackets where they should be used.

1   We have known each other for ten no, twelve years.

2   My punk friend Liz the one with the blue hair has four earrings in each ear.

3   Give me back my homework right now or else.

Worksheet 15   Rule 8 (Page 14)

WORKING IN PAIRS

Each sentence below contains one little mistake in the use of speech marks. Correct the mistake and on the line in front of the sentence write the letter of the rule you used to make the correction.

1 _____ "We're going to make a film at the club" said Benj.

2 _____ Jon said, "The most important character is a detective." "I would love to be the detective." "I'm a natural detective-type."

3 _____ Benj replied, "sorry, chum, we've already chosen your part for you."

4 _____ "Jon mumbled, yeah I can guess. I'm going to be the corpse."

5 _____ "Nope" his friend answered "you're going to be the alsation."

Worksheet 16   Rule 9 (Page 15)

GROUP EXERCISE WORK

The letter that follows was sent by a child to a friend in hospital. It has several mistakes in the use of capitals. Make the corrections, and above each put the letter of the rule you used to make the correction.

Dear Janice,

I hope you are enjoying your stay at northwick park hospital. we're probably all more conscious of the green cross code now. It was a pity you missed the trip to paris. We went to all the expected places: the Eiffel tower, The louvre, Arc de triomphe. my preference was for Sacré coeur at montmartre, and i think it would have been yours too.

Our new french teacher, Mr duval, who is very active in greenpeace, kept pointing out how pollution has affected Notre dame and other churches.

On saturday, jean, jenny and i are going to the Watford palace to see 'Cider with rosie'. I wish you could come with us. however, we will come to see you soon. Avril says, 'keep your chin up; think of all the school you're getting out of!'

                    Love,   *Nina*

Worksheet 17   Affect, Effect (Page 17)

WORK THESE THROUGH

In the following sentences, write the correct form of the word to fill the blank.

1   The _____ of some insecticides is to kill off bees and butterflies.

2   Confidence _____ how well you do at school.

3   The music I listen to _____ the way I behave.

4   Mark got a good _____ with the stage-lighting.

5   Do onions _____ your eyes?

6   Football violence has had a bad _____ on attendance at matches.

7   A big volcano can _____ the climate around the world.

8   The amount of study you do _____ exam results.

Worksheet 18   Amount, Number (Page 18)

WORK THESE THROUGH

In the following sentences, cross out the expression that is incorrect.

1   Could you lend me a number/an amount of sheets of paper?

2   A large amount/number of concrete was used to build the dam.

3   The clubhouse was packed with a large number/amount of players.

4   The number/amount of ways to solve the problem confused the student.

5   A great number/amount of nuclear waste is buried in the sea.

6   A small number/amount of sugar was spilled on the table.

7   The number/amount of records in your Beatles collection is impressive.

8   A number/An amount of girl guides were standing outside the church.

Worksheet 19   Between, Among (Page 19)

WORK THESE THROUGH

In each of the following decide whether among *or* between *is correct and fill in the blanks.*

1   _____ the crowd were several girls with pink hair.

2   Mum and Dad can arrange the baby-sitting _____ themselves.

3   Let's keep the secret _____ you and me.

4   The fire in the stadium was one _____ several disasters this year.

5   Deal these cards _____ the five players.

6   You can share these sweets _____ you and your brother.

7   The paper and pens were distributed _____ the exam candidates.

Worksheet 20   Breath, Breathe (Page 20)

WORK THESE THROUGH

Write the correct word in each blank.

1   A little _____ of relief escaped from her lips.

2   It is good for your health to _____ deeply.

3   You can fall ill if you _____ in asbestos dust.

4   He said he would hold his _____ until he fainted.

5   But he soon began to _____ quite freely.

6   When she walked in, it was like a _____ of fresh air.

7   There was not a _____ of air on that summer's day.

8   We could _____ easily after the principal had passed.

Worksheet 21   Continual, Continuous (Page 21)

WORK THESE THROUGH

Write the correct word in each blank.

1   The _____ rain lasted for 24 hours.

2   He is _____ly asking his father for money.

3   Many old people retire to Italy for the _____ sunshine.

4   In winter, he suffers from _____ colds and coughs.

5   In the classroom there was a _____ murmur.

6   Hilary's friends ring her up _____ly.

7   The _____ buzzing of the bees lulled Sam to sleep.

8   Ranji's brother changed jobs _____ly.

9   The _____ sound of muzak distracted the musician.

Worksheet 22   Farther, Further (Page 25)

WORK THESE THROUGH

Write the appropriate word in each blank.

1   We walked several miles _____ than you.

2   Joey could see the building _____ in the distance.

3   We can make no _____ progress on this play.

4   I live _____ from London than you do.

5   There will be a _____ discussion about bullying next week.

6   I could get no _____ with arrangements for the party.

7   The Tower of London is _____ than you think.

Worksheet 23   Fewer, Less (Page 25)

WORK THESE THROUGH

Write the correct word in each blank.

1   There are _____ girls than boys in the class.

2   We've had _____ hours of sunshine this year than last.

3   We've certainly not had _____ rain though.

4   The students collected _____ money for the charity this year.

5   _____ people went to the air display than expected.

6   We are expecting _____ absences this month.

7   You should drink _____ fizzy drinks.

8   I got _____ work from you this term than ever before.

9   I wish there were _____ nasty news items on TV and
        _____ violence in the world.

Worksheet 24   Hardly, Scarcely (Page 26)

WORK THESE THROUGH

Put a cross after the incorrect sentences.

1   We didn't have hardly any supper last night. ____

2   We had hardly any supper last night. ____

3   The neighbours had scarcely been out an hour when the roof fell
        in. ____

4   The neighbours hadn't scarcely been out an hour when the roof fell
        in. ____

Worksheet 25   Imply, Infer (Page 27)

WORK THESE THROUGH

In the following sentences, cross out the inappropriate word.

1   Your smile implies/infers you understood the joke.

2   I imply/infer from your remarks that you want me to leave.

3   Are you implying/inferring that you got a new bike for your birthday?

4   Robert has implied/inferred that you are holding a grudge.

5   We can imply/infer from these statistics that unemployment is
        increasing.

6   Ramesh implied/inferred from the teacher's remarks that he had made
        top marks.

7   The teacher implied/inferred that the maths would be difficult for me
        to understand.

Worksheet 26   Its, It's (Page 28)

WORK THESE THROUGH

Write the correct word in each blank.

1   _____ only a few days until my birthday.

2   Maybe _____ too late to buy tickets.

3   The chair has lost _____ leg.

4   The dog was frightened of _____ master.

5   Do you know if _____ the 21st today?

6   I miss _____ big eyes and fluffy tail.

7   _____ possible to get to the top of Tower Bridge now.

8   _____ worth going to the top of the bridge, just for
        _____ view.

Worksheet 27   Lose, Loose (Page 30)

WORK THESE THROUGH

Some of the following sentences use lose *and* loose *correctly. Put a cross by the incorrect sentences.*

1   Please don't loose my place in the book. ____

2   I might lose my ring because it is too loose on my finger. ____

3   These lose trousers are really comfortable. ____

4   The screws in this chair are all loose. ____

5   You can count on Atul to lose his homework every time. ____

6   Monica must not be let lose in a sweet shop. ____

7   One thing is sure: you can't loose what you haven't got. ____

Worksheet 28   Lying, Laying (Page 30)

WORK THESE THROUGH

In each of the blanks write the correct form.

1   Stop _____ around; do your homework.

2   Mother isn't well; she's _____ down at the moment.

3   The last time I saw your jacket it was _____ over the back of the sofa.

4   Marie was _____ the table while I was _____ in front of the TV.

5   The principal is always _____ down the law to us.

6   You'll get sunstroke, _____ out in the sun like that.

7   My brother is always _____ bets on who will get to school first.

Worksheet 29   Myself, Himself, Herself, Itself, Yourself, Themselves (Page 31)

WORK THESE THROUGH

*Each of the following sentences is correct. After each sentence write down the letter of the rule **a**, **b**, or **c** that has been used.*

1   Jason reminded himself that he had a dental appointment.   (   )

2   The pupils themselves objected to too much freedom.   (   )

3   I myself will deliver the note to the principal.   (   )

4   She saw herself reflected in the store window.   (   )

5   You can blame yourself for your bad test result.   (   )

6   Mother asked you herself to tidy the kitchen.   (   )

7   We considered ourselves lucky to be alive.   (   )

8   The dog shook itself, showering everyone with water.   (   )

Worksheet 30   Off, Of (Page 33)

WORK THESE THROUGH

Write the correct word in each blank.

1   He climbed to the top _____ the hill.

2   She fell _____ her bike.

3   I hope to get _____ report by next week.

4   There were three hours _____ sunlight left.

5   Three _____ us will arrive at 8.00 p.m. precisely.

6   I was taught maths by the better _____ the two teachers.

7   This dress had ten pounds marked _____ the original price.

8   Which _____ these records do you prefer?

Worksheet 31   Passed, Past (Page 34)

WORK THESE THROUGH

In each of the blanks write the correct form.

1   The trembling postman _____ the vicious dog.

2   Carol lives just _____ the letter box.

3   Mother says the _____ is best forgotten.

4   The ugly cardigan was _____ from relative to relative.

5   She walked _____ the bakery with her eyes closed.

6   I will forget my _____ mistakes and start again.

7   John _____ the chips to his brother.

8   It is way _____ tea time.

Worksheet 32   Practice, Practise (Page 35)

WORK THESE THROUGH

*Write in the correct form of the word. At the end of each sentence, write between the brackets whether you used rule **a** or rule **b**.*

1   The lawyer decided to sell his _____.   (   )

2   Two weeks in France is worth a year of _____ in the classroom.   (   )

3   I _____ the drums every evening between 6.00 and 7.00.   (   )

4   Religious _____ has changed over the last hundred years.   (   )

5   Your table-tennis will improve if you _____ regularly.   (   )

6   I wonder if the cricket coach knows how often I _____ bowling.   (   )

Worksheet 33   Quiet, Quite (Page 36)

WORK THESE THROUGH

Write the correct word in each blank.

1   I am _____ glad to see the end of that biology course.

2   Ranjiv was _____ well-informed about computers.

3   When Mum spoke to him she sounded _____ annoyed.

4   Most people prefer the _____ life.

5   Others like _____ a lot of excitement.

6   Karen is _____ prepared to give up sports to prepare for
        GCSEs.

7   If you don't keep _____, I will ask you to leave.

8   He was _____ helpless with laughter.

Worksheet 34   Than, Then (Page 37)

WORK THESE THROUGH

Cross out the incorrect word in each sentence.

1   The children will be here later then/than expected.

2   Meeta is more beautiful then/than her sister.

3   Then/Than he handed me the map.

4   Peter's temperature was higher today then/than yesterday.

5   His English teacher then/than refused to re-mark his paper.

6   First I will go swimming then/than I'll meet you at the cinema.

7   Mary was better at maths then/than she was at physics.

8   He then/than stood up and stormed out of the room.

Worksheet 35 Their, There, They're (Page 37)

WORK THESE THROUGH

Write in the correct form of the word.

1 The children put _____ shoes in the dustbin.

2 I wonder if _____ coming to the match.

3 _____ were ten green bottles on the wall.

4 I'll write to Merryl when she gets _____.

5 My sisters will get _____ results tomorrow.

6 Pay for the theatre ticket when you get _____.

7 The workmen say _____ cutting down those trees for firewood.

8 Those houses have lost all _____ roof-tiles.

9 Unfortunately, in that team _____ all bad losers.

Worksheet 36   Where, Were (Page 40)

WORK THESE THROUGH

Tick the correct sentence in each pair.

1a   There where terrible winds last night.
1b   There were terrible winds last night.

2a   Peter knew where to look for my keys.
2b   Peter knew were to look for my keys.

3a   The French boys were here two years ago.
3b   The French boys where here two years ago.

4a   Six teachers where absent today.
4b   Six teachers were absent today.

5a   The taxi driver didn't know were the hospital was.
5b   The taxi driver didn't know where the hospital was.

6a   I went to visit the house where I was born.
6b   I went to visit the house were I was born.

7a   Ketan wondered were all the prizes where.
7b   Ketan wondered where all the prizes were.

8a   What would you do if you where me?
8b   What would you do if you were me?

9a   The reporters were not allowed to see the President.
9b   The reporters where not allowed to see the President.

Worksheet 37   Who, Which, That (Page 41)

WORK THESE THROUGH

Five of the following sentences are correct. Tick the correct ones. Correct the wrong ones.

1   The candidate which is most popular is Sangita Patel.

2   The dog who bit my brother has been put down.

3   He lost the pen that his mother had given him.

4   I like cars in which you can go at 120 m.p.h.

5   The car that we went to Birmingham in was a Mercedes.

6   Nat Kelly likes people which are cleverer than he is.

7   There are few people who are as clever as him.

8   Her shoes which are just like mine are two sizes larger.

9   The cats who live next door have practically moved in on us.

Worksheet 38   Whose, Who's (Page 41)

WORK THESE THROUGH

*Write the correct word in each blank. In the brackets at the end of each sentence, write the letter **a** or **b** of the rule you followed.*

1   Everyone _____ been to Disneyland has loved it.   (   )

2   _____ that lady with your mother?   (   )

3   The person _____ to blame isn't here.   (   )

4   That's the boy _____ dog got run over.   (   )

5   Is Timmy the pupil _____ moving to Paris?   (   )

6   _____ plimsolls were taken from the classroom?   (   )

7   I wonder _____ coming to the party.   (   )

Worksheet 39   Your, You're (Page 42)

WORK THESE THROUGH

Write the correct form of the word in each blank.

1   I hope _____ ready for the maths test.

2   _____ always the last one to arrive.

3   What is _____ contribution to the assembly programme?

4   Meg would like to borrow _____ English book.

5   _____ bedroom looks like a tip.

6   _____ going to tidy it up before you go out.

7   This is _____ last chance to get a raffle ticket.

8   If _____ annoyed, please say so.

9   Would _____ wellingtons fit Sandra?

Worksheet 40   Rule 1 (Page 44)

GROUP EXERCISE WORK

Make each of the sentences 'possible' or 'unlikely' by crossing out the inappropriate words. An example has been done for you.

      ✓   (possible)   If Eddie comes/came by 8.00, we will/would be on time.

1   (unlikely)   If a pop-star sings/sang at our morning assembly, there will/would be chaos.

2   (possible)   If the snow stops/stopped, Dad will/would drive to London.

3   (unlikely)   If I play/played cricket like Ian Botham, I will/would make the school team.

4   (possible)   If I ask/asked to stay out until 1.00 a.m., Mother will/would not let me.

5   (possible)   If Ketan joins/joined the tennis club, he will/would win all the tournaments.

6   (unlikely)   If England wins/won the ashes, we will/would get a day off school.

7   (possible)   If my sister gets/got a job modelling, she will/would be unbearable to live with.

8   (unlikely)   If Margaret Thatcher joins/joined the S.D.P., no one will/would believe it.

9   (unlikely)   If that dog bites/bit me, I will/would sue the owner.

Worksheet 41   Rule 3 (Page 47)

GROUP EXERCISE WORK

Circle the correct form of the verb.

1   I (go/goes) to the cinema at least once a week.

2   But Errol (go/goes) about four times a week.

3   He (know/knows) almost every actor and pop star.

4   His mum (think/thinks) he (spend/spends) too much time at the cinema.

5   His dad (say/says) he (don't/doesn't) mind.

6   Errol (hangs/hang) around cinemas, but not around discos.

7   Errol's dad (hate/hates) discos.

8   He (imagines/imagine) people get in fights there.

9   His parents really (wants/want) Errol to hang around libraries.

Worksheet 42   Rule 5 (Page 48)

GROUP EXERCISE WORK

Complete these five sentences first by yourself; then compare your work with a partner's and agree on the correct answer.

1   *The Fly* is the _____ (frightening) film I've ever seen.

2   Of the two I'd prefer the _____ (big) piece of cake.

3   Marie is the _____ (beautiful) girl in the fifth form.

4   The maths homework was _____ (simple) than the physics.

5   John is _____ (helpful) around the house than his sister is.

Worksheet 43   Suggestion 2 (Page 52)

WORKING IN PAIRS

Circle the parts of the words below that you think would cause you or another student trouble. Then compare your list with your partner's to see if you have both circled the same letters. Next to the word write down what must be remembered to keep the spelling from going wrong. The first two words have been done for you.

WORD	PROBLEM
a c c o m m o d a t i o n	2 c's + o, 2 m's + o
r e c o g n i s e	g in the middle
d e c i d e	
a l c o h o l	
l i g h t n i n g	
e n v i r o n m e n t	
p r o b a b l y	
r e m e m b e r	

When you have studied these words, close the book and with your partner recall and write down as many of the words as you can. Circle on your own spellings the problem places. Check your spelling against each other, then against the book.

Worksheet 44   Suggestion 3 (Page 52)

WORKING IN PAIRS 1

*Circle the ie/ei in the words below. Next to the words write the reason **1**, **2**, or **3** for the use. The first three words have been done for you.*

WORD	REASON FOR YOUR CHOICE OF SPELLING
br(ie)f	(1) i before e
w(ei)gh	(3) ei pronounced other than ee
dec(ei)ve	(2) ei after c
field	_____
eight	_____
height	_____
heir	_____
pier	_____
relief	_____
receive	_____

WORKING IN PAIRS 2

Working with a partner, decide whether to put ie *or* ei *in the blank spaces below; then in the brackets write **1**, **2**, or **3** to show which part of the rhyme you used.*

conc__ __t ( )   for__ __gn ( )

r__ __gn ( )   th__ __f ( )

v__ __n ( )

Worksheet 45 Suggestion 6: Rule 3 (Page 54)

WORKING IN PAIRS

*The following words are spelled correctly. Circle the letter before the y, change the y as necessary and write the plural correctly. Working with your partner say whether you used **a** or **b** from Rule 3 to spell the plural. Then write down the rule next to the word. The first one has been done for you.*

	WORD/PLURAL	RULE
1	lorry / lorries	change y to i if a consonant comes before the y + ending
2	storey /	_____
3	hobby /	_____
4	monkey /	_____
5	city /	_____
6	boy /	_____
7	chimney /	_____
8	factory /	_____
9	enemy /	_____